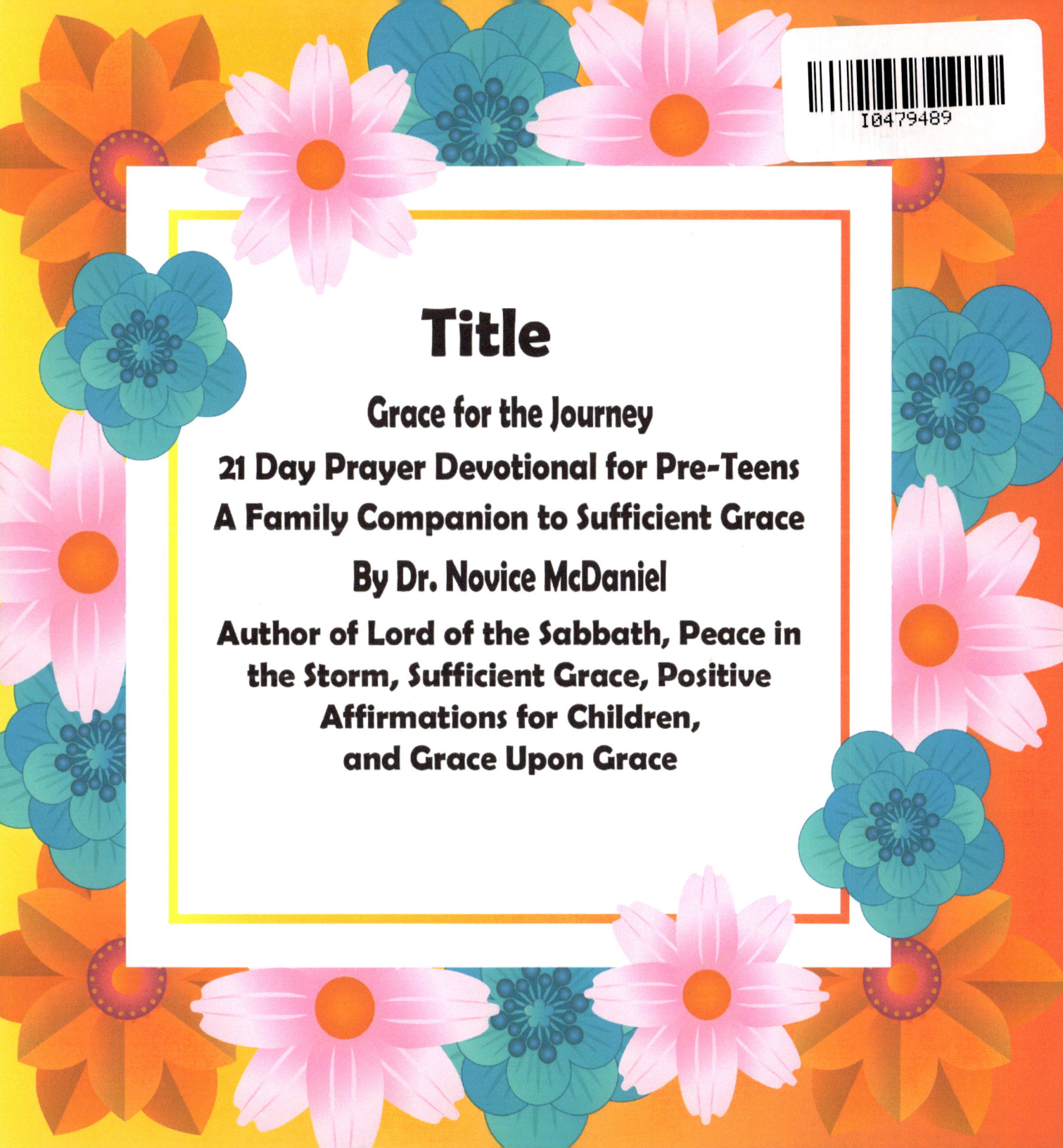

# Title

### Grace for the Journey
### 21 Day Prayer Devotional for Pre-Teens
### A Family Companion to Sufficient Grace

### By Dr. Novice McDaniel

### Author of Lord of the Sabbath, Peace in the Storm, Sufficient Grace, Positive Affirmations for Children, and Grace Upon Grace

# Dedication

This book is dedicated to all children everywhere. It was inspired by all the children of my family and friends known and unknown. They all inspire me to be a positive influence and I desire that this book will be a blessing in their lives, drawing them closer to God.

My prayer is that they will all grow up knowing and demonstrating that they are special, they are loved, and they can be all that God has created them to be!

# Introduction

Introducing "Grace for the Journey: A 21 Day Prayer Devotional for Pre-Teens" and a family companion to Sufficient Grace. This book is designed to inspire and guide young hearts, inviting pre-teens to explore their faith and deepen their connection with God through prayer. As they pour out their hopes, dreams, and concerns, they will uncover the power of prayer and experience the comfort of knowing that God is always listening. Join us on this extraordinary journey of self-discovery, faith, and prayer. "Grace for the Journey" is the key for unlocking the transformative power of prayer in the lives of pre-teens everywhere.

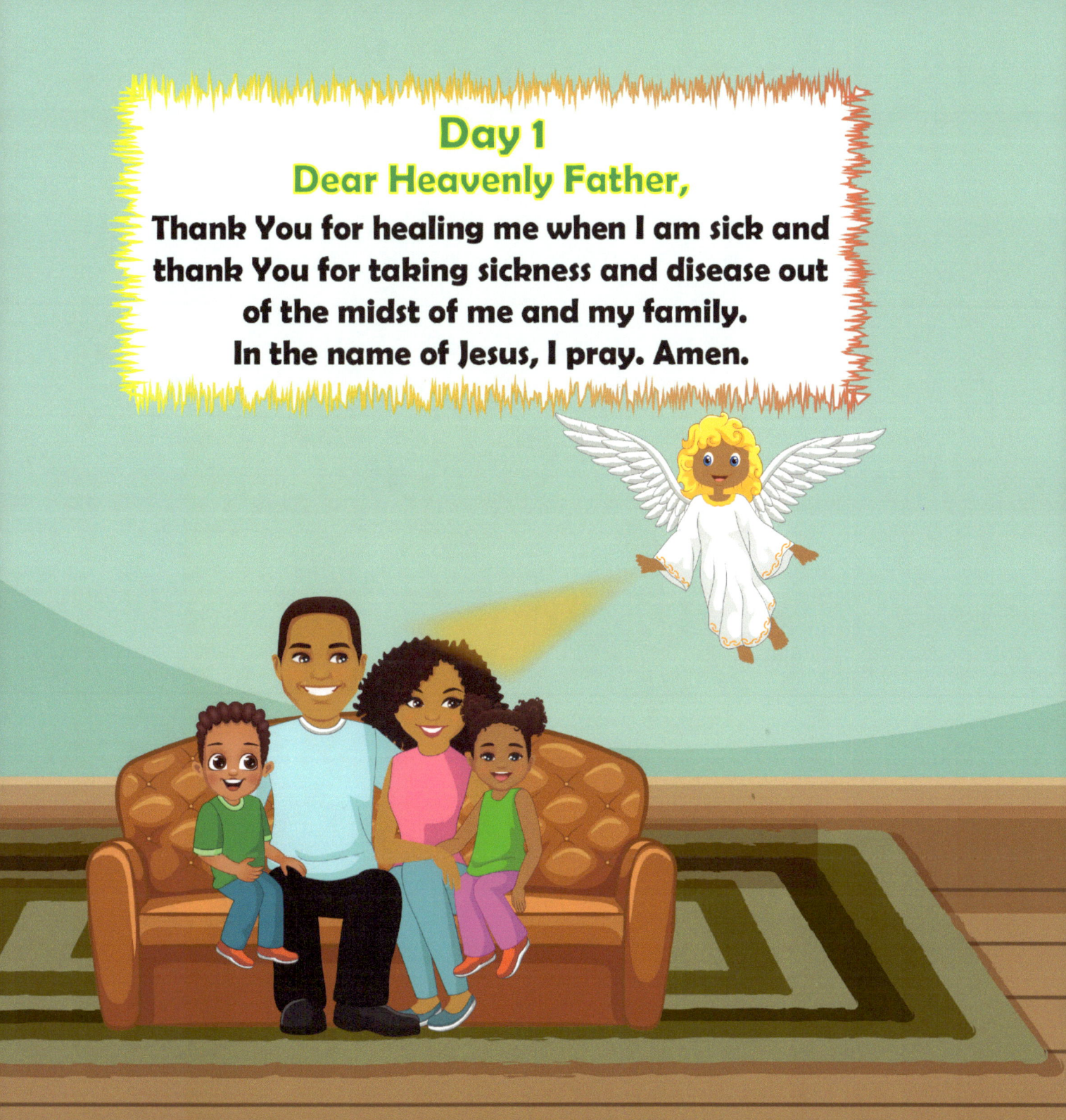

# Day 1
## Dear Heavenly Father,

Thank You for healing me when I am sick and thank You for taking sickness and disease out of the midst of me and my family.
In the name of Jesus, I pray. Amen.

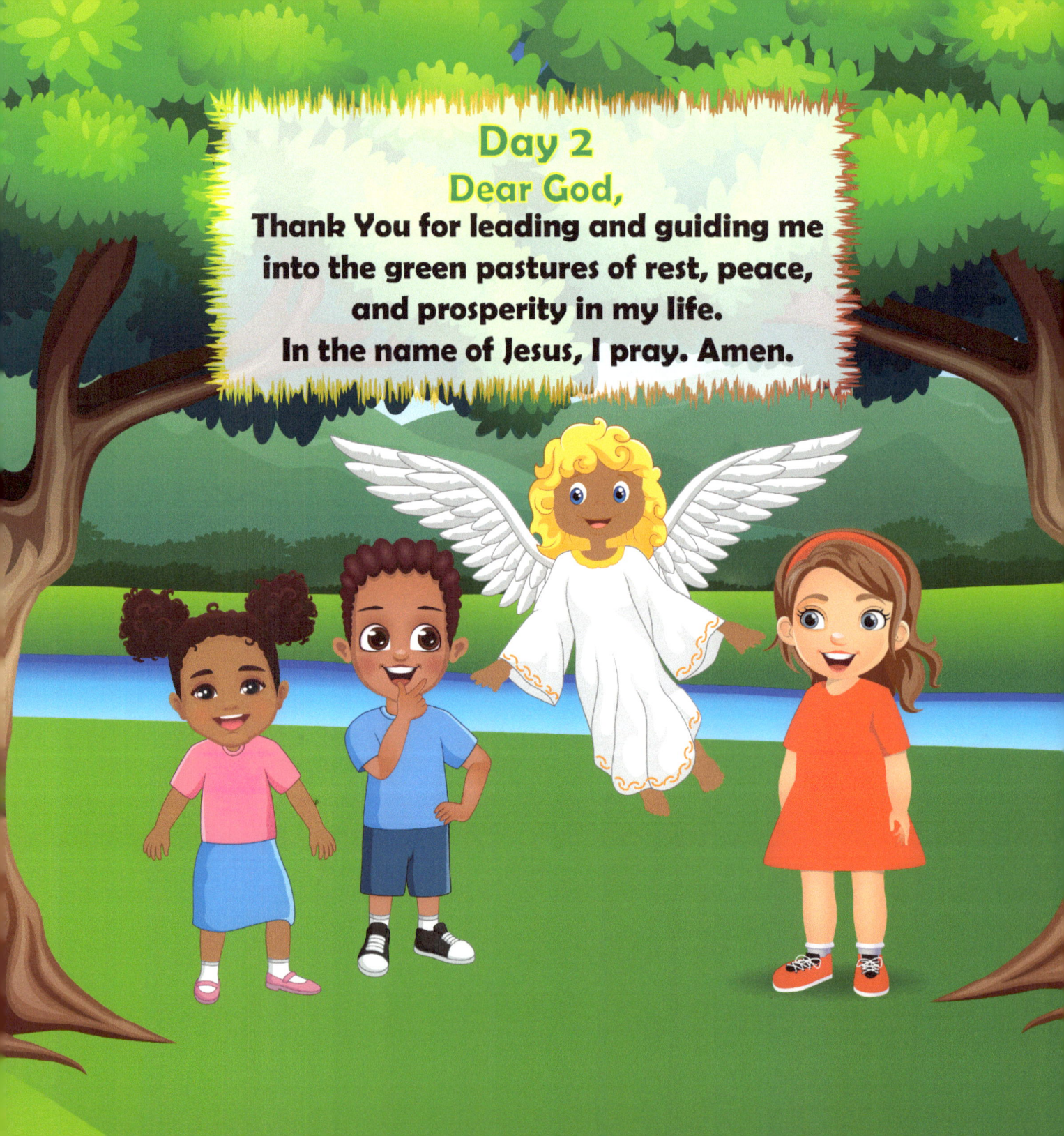

# Day 2
## Dear God,
Thank You for leading and guiding me into the green pastures of rest, peace, and prosperity in my life.
In the name of Jesus, I pray. Amen.

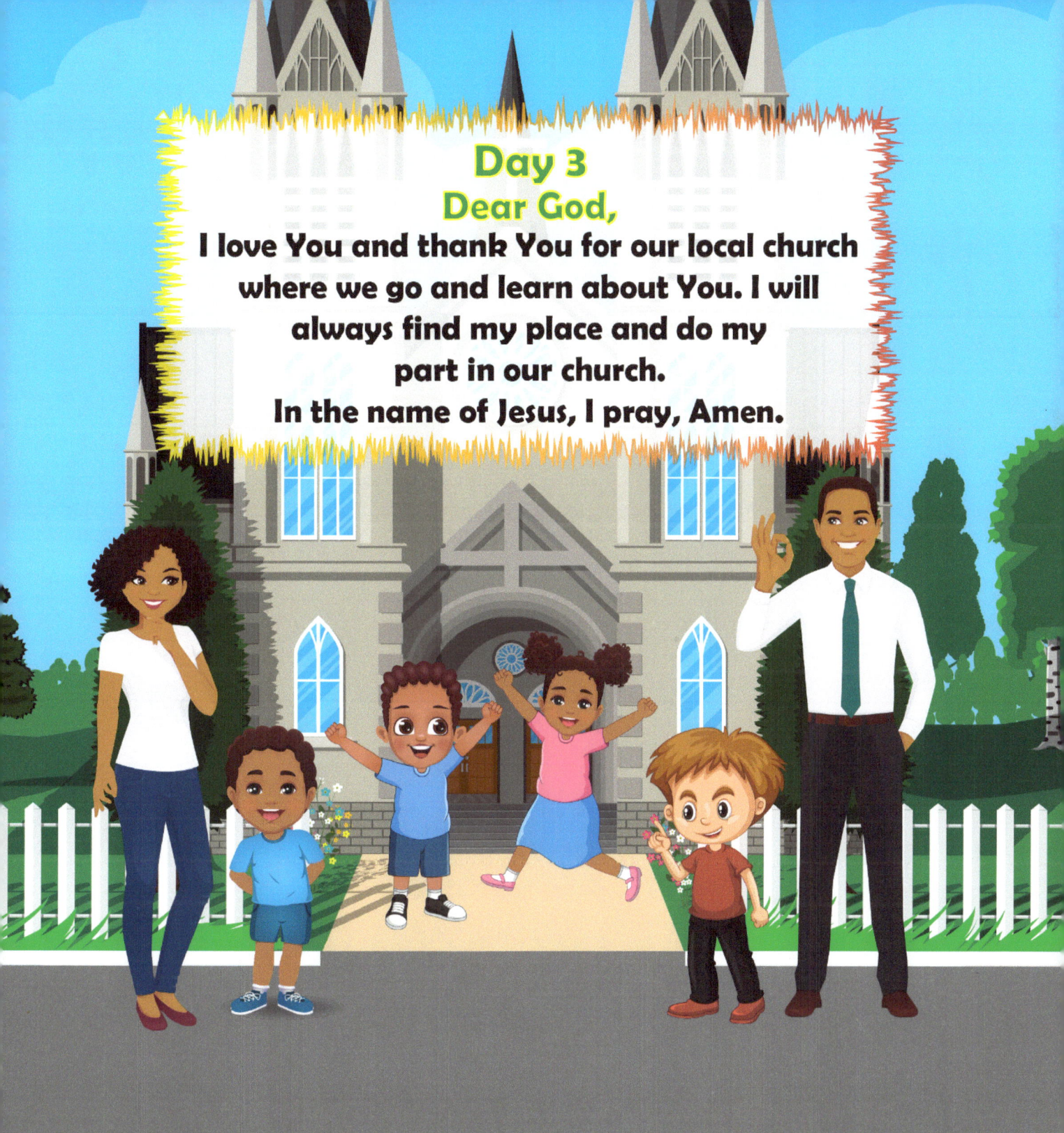

**Day 3**
**Dear God,**
I love You and thank You for our local church where we go and learn about You. I will always find my place and do my part in our church.
In the name of Jesus, I pray, Amen.

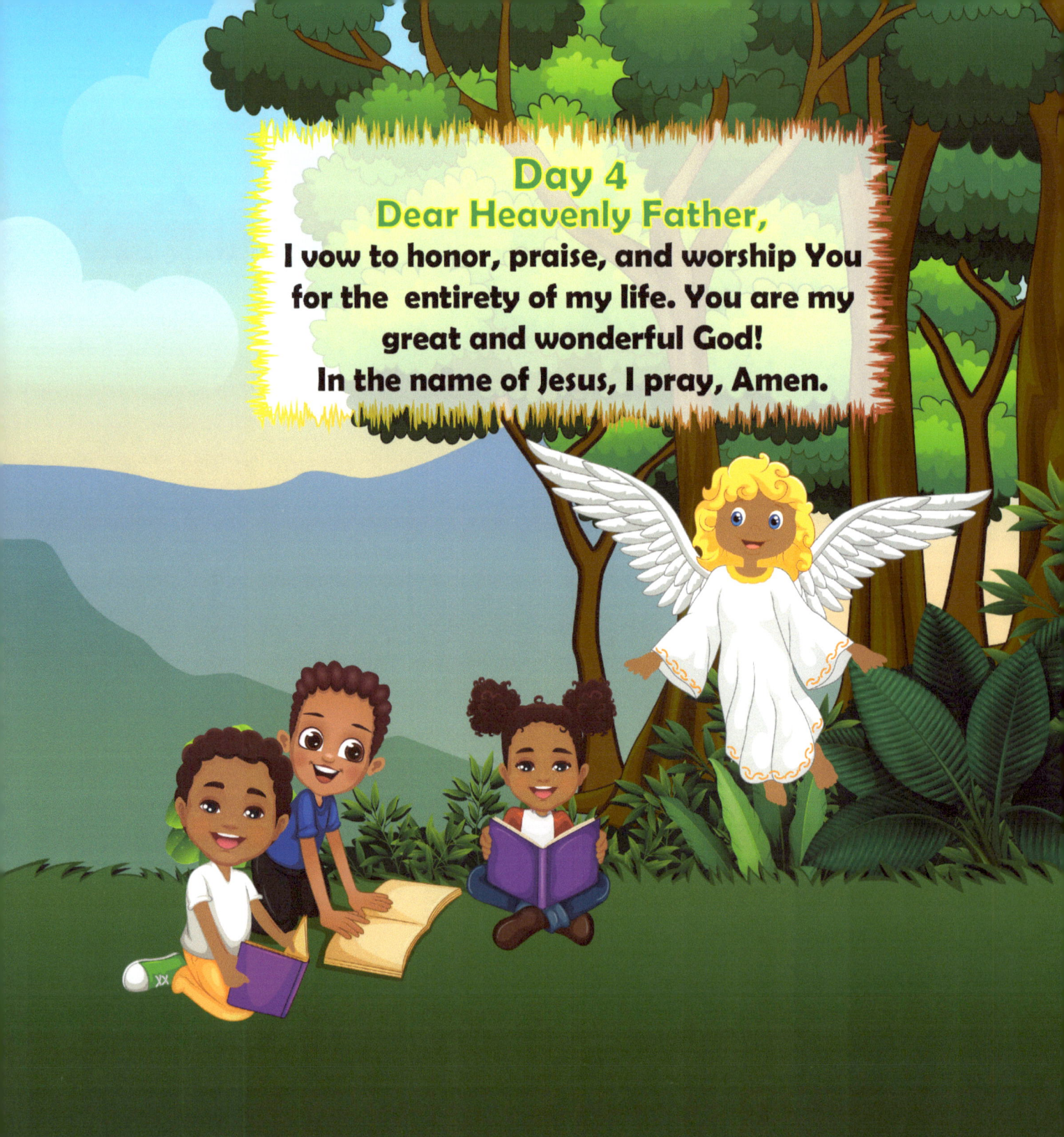

# Day 4
## Dear Heavenly Father,

I vow to honor, praise, and worship You for the entirety of my life. You are my great and wonderful God!
In the name of Jesus, I pray, Amen.

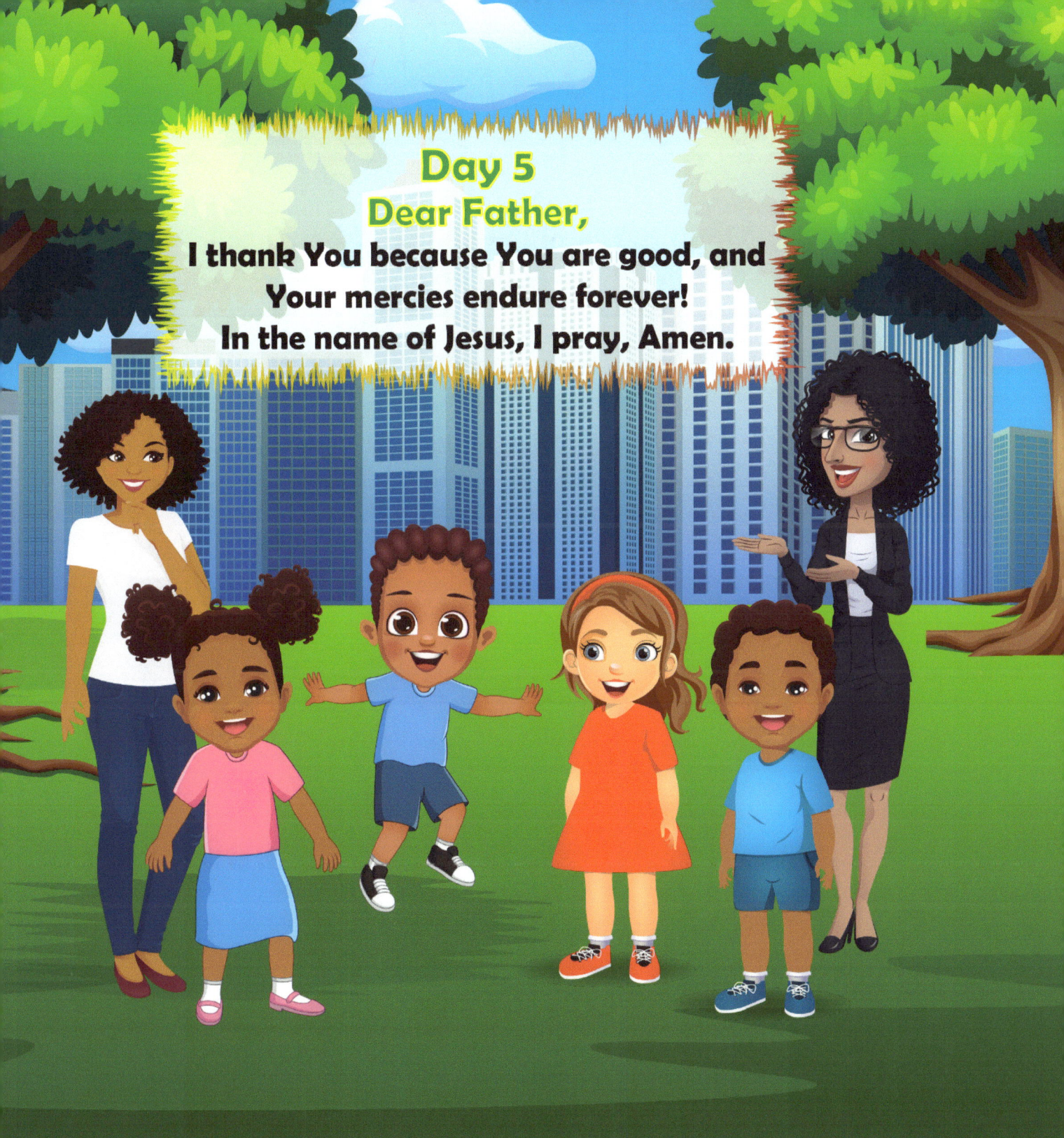

**Day 5**
**Dear Father,**
I thank You because You are good, and
Your mercies endure forever!
In the name of Jesus, I pray, Amen.

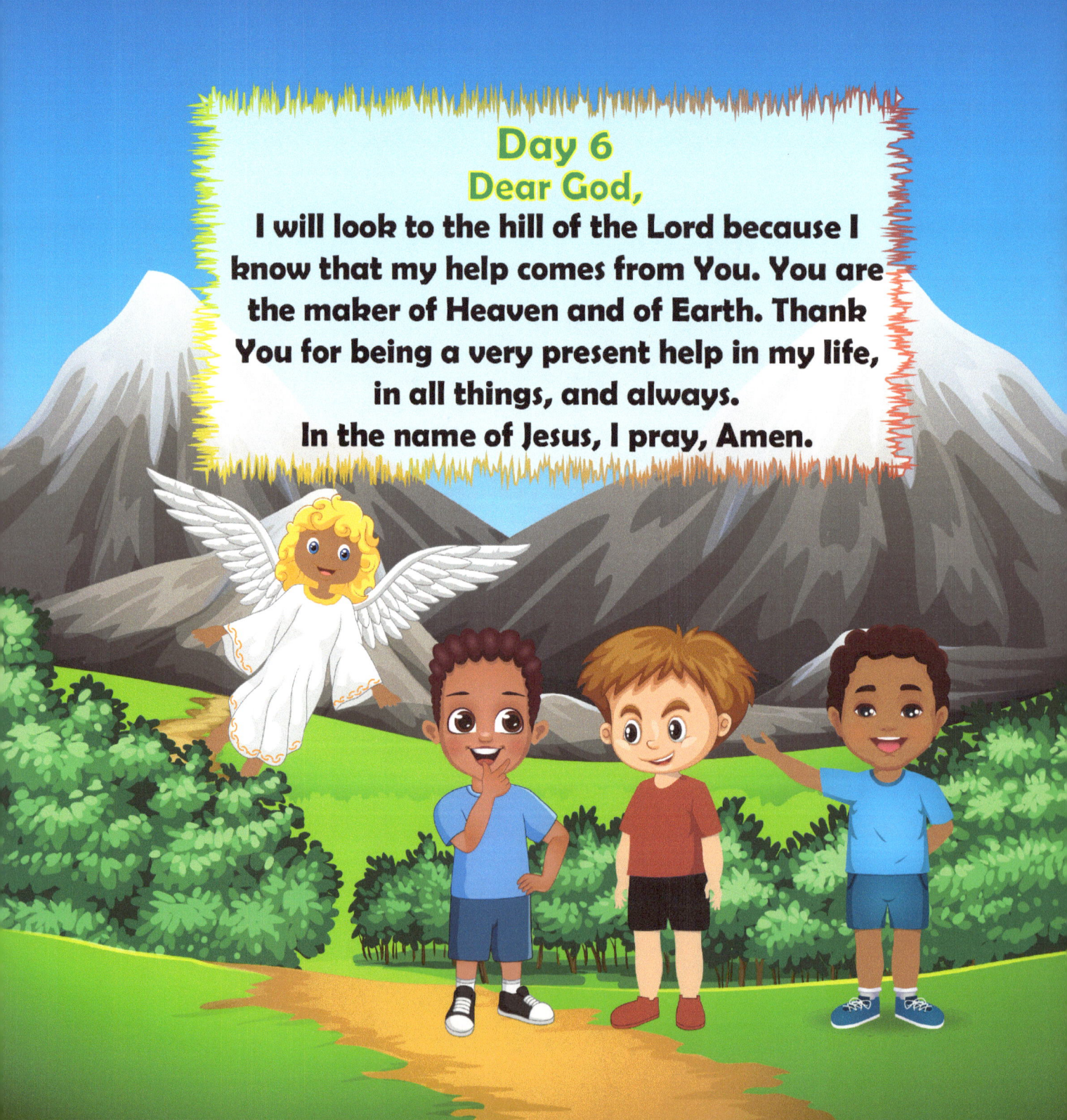

# Day 6
## Dear God,

I will look to the hill of the Lord because I know that my help comes from You. You are the maker of Heaven and of Earth. Thank You for being a very present help in my life, in all things, and always.
In the name of Jesus, I pray, Amen.

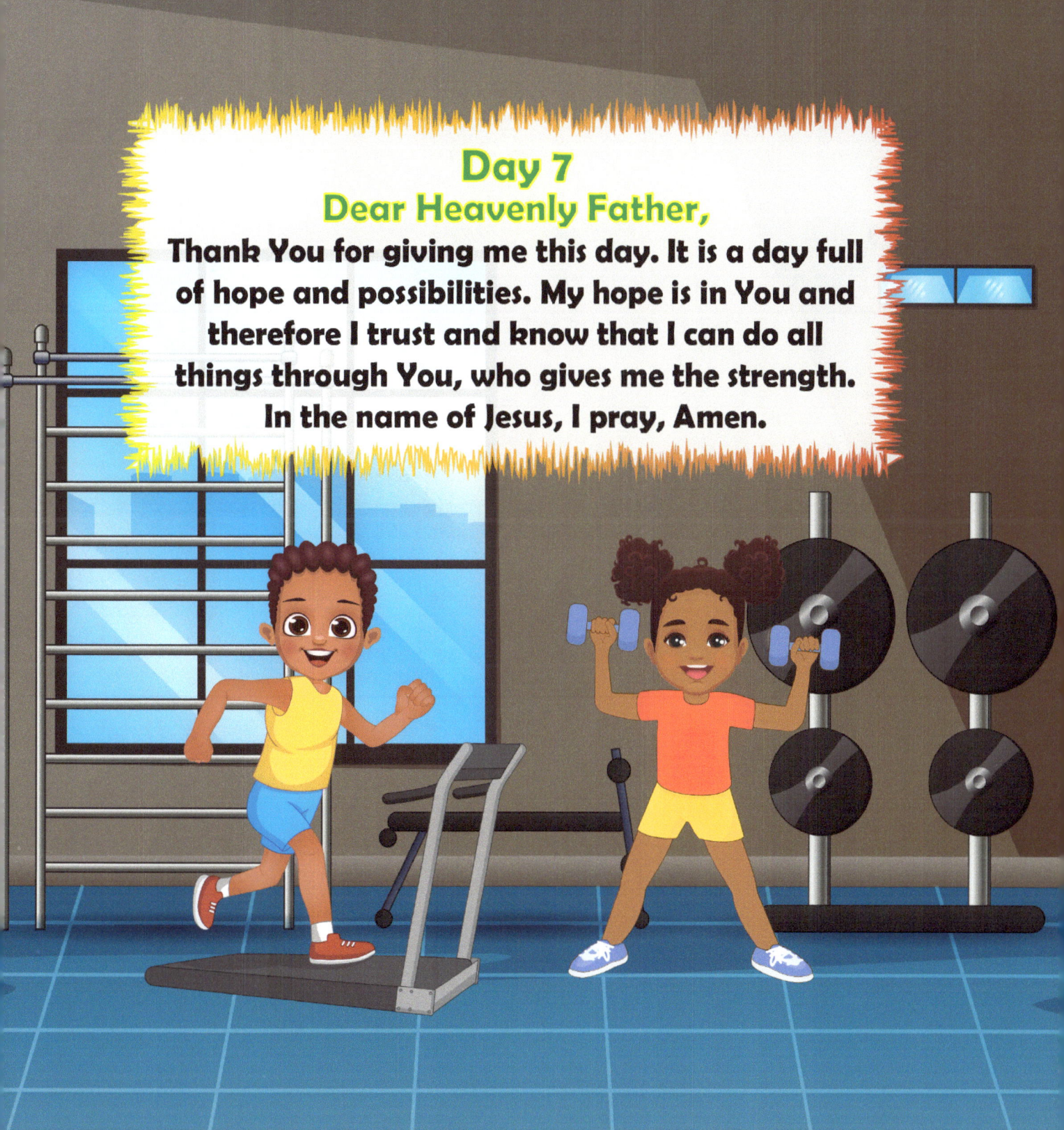

**Day 7**
**Dear Heavenly Father,**
Thank You for giving me this day. It is a day full of hope and possibilities. My hope is in You and therefore I trust and know that I can do all things through You, who gives me the strength. In the name of Jesus, I pray, Amen.

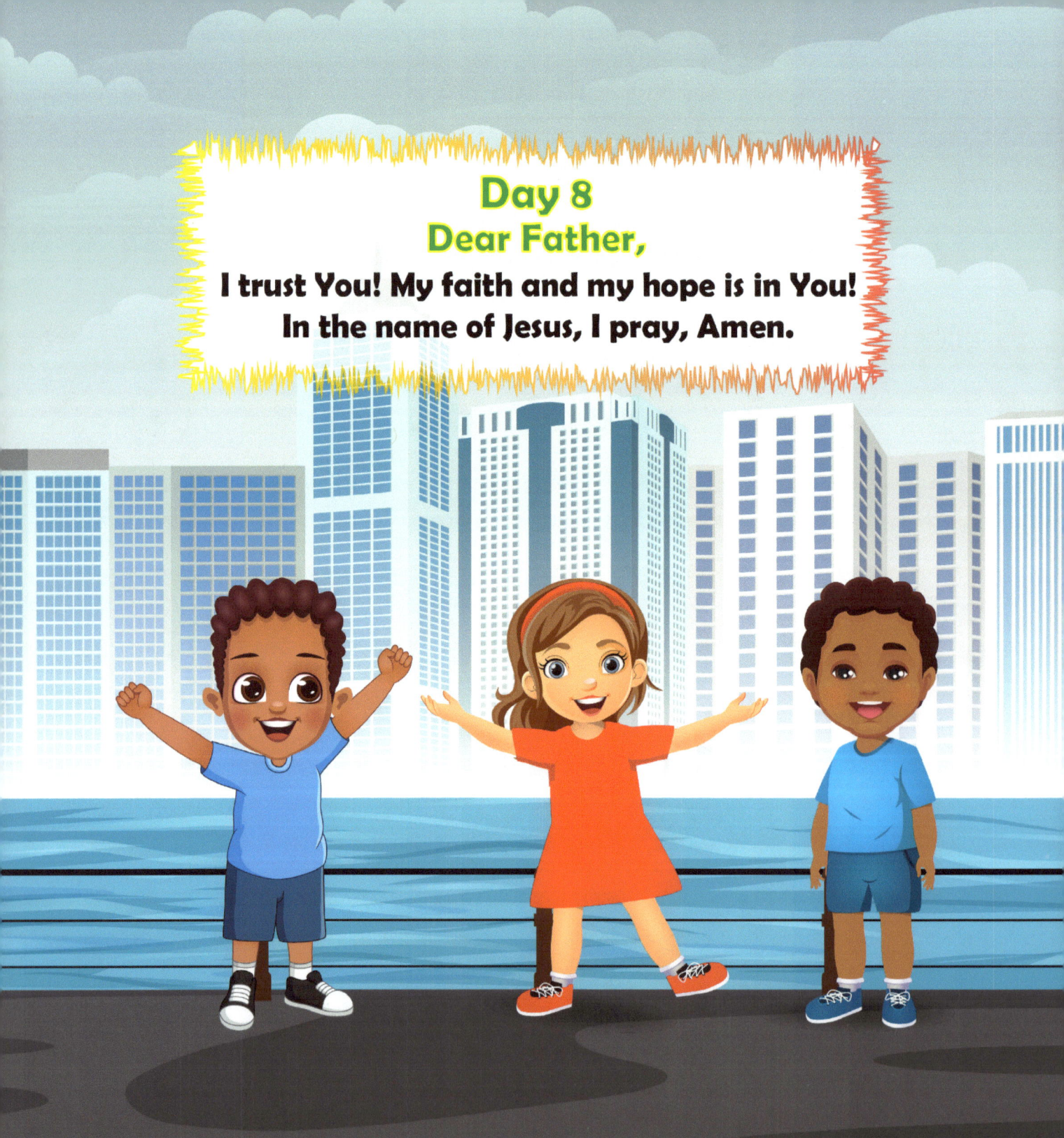

**Day 8**
**Dear Father,**
I trust You! My faith and my hope is in You!
In the name of Jesus, I pray, Amen.

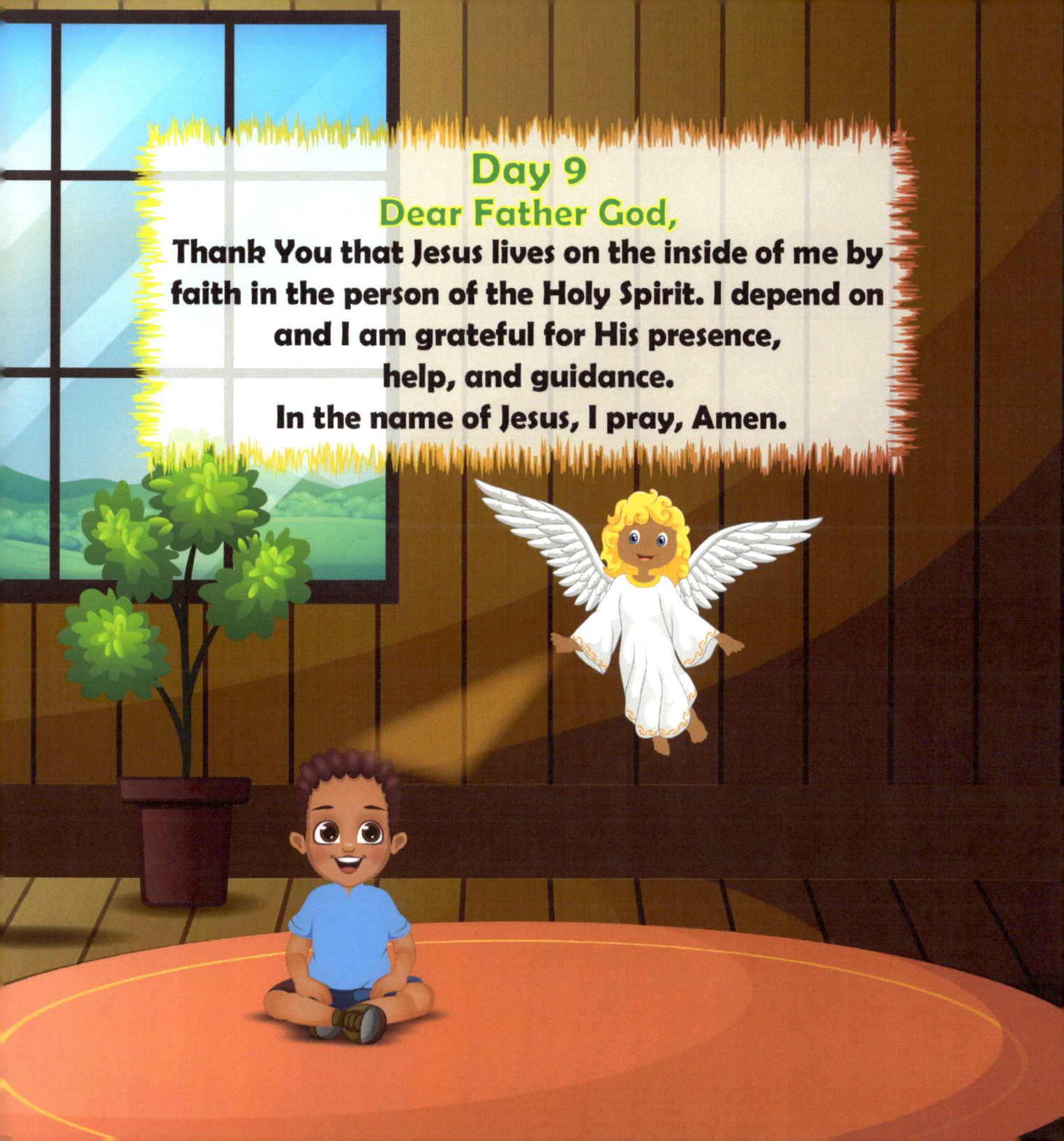

**Day 9**
**Dear Father God,**
Thank You that Jesus lives on the inside of me by faith in the person of the Holy Spirit. I depend on and I am grateful for His presence, help, and guidance.
In the name of Jesus, I pray, Amen.

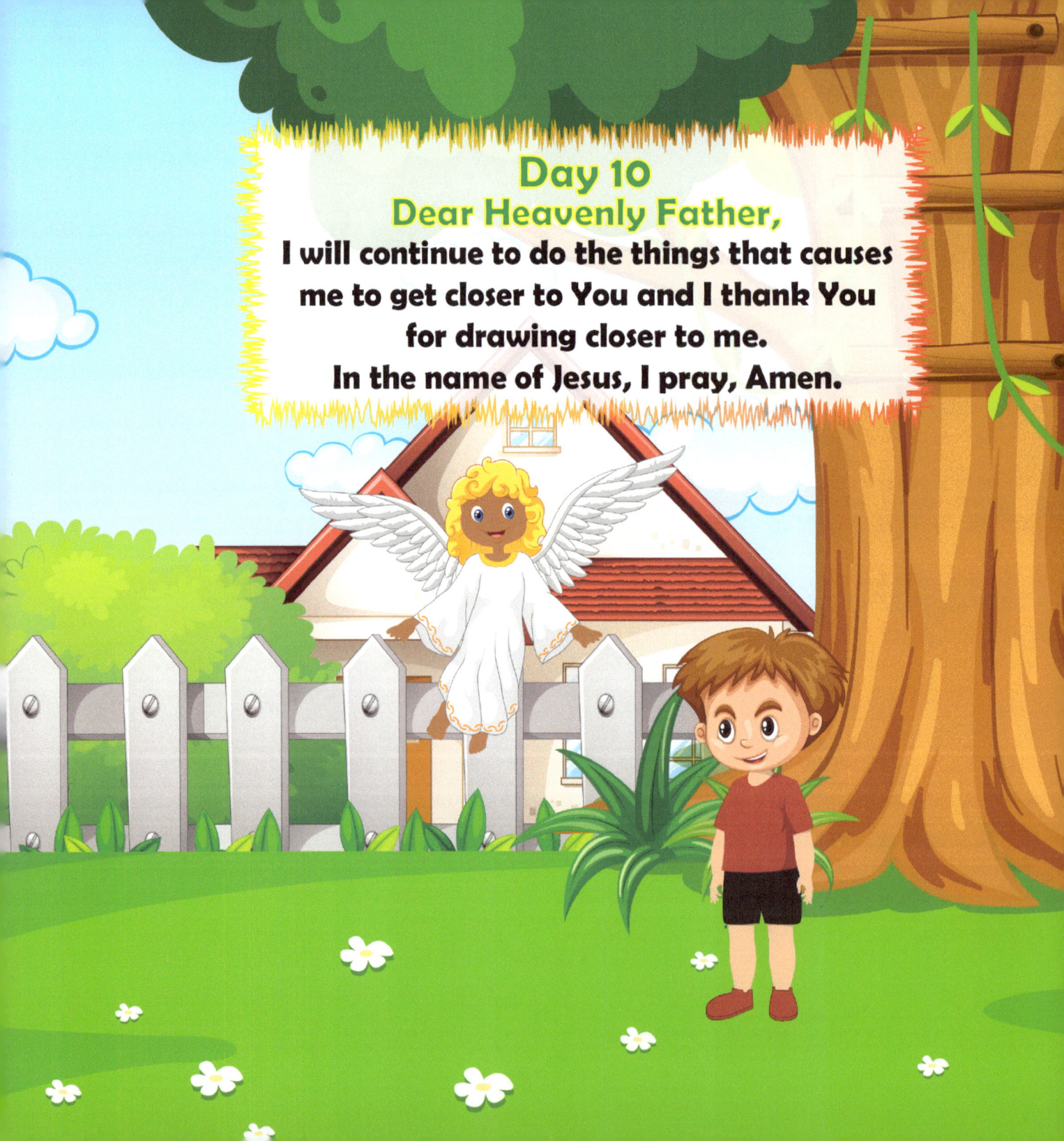

**Day 10**
**Dear Heavenly Father,**
I will continue to do the things that causes me to get closer to You and I thank You for drawing closer to me.
In the name of Jesus, I pray, Amen.

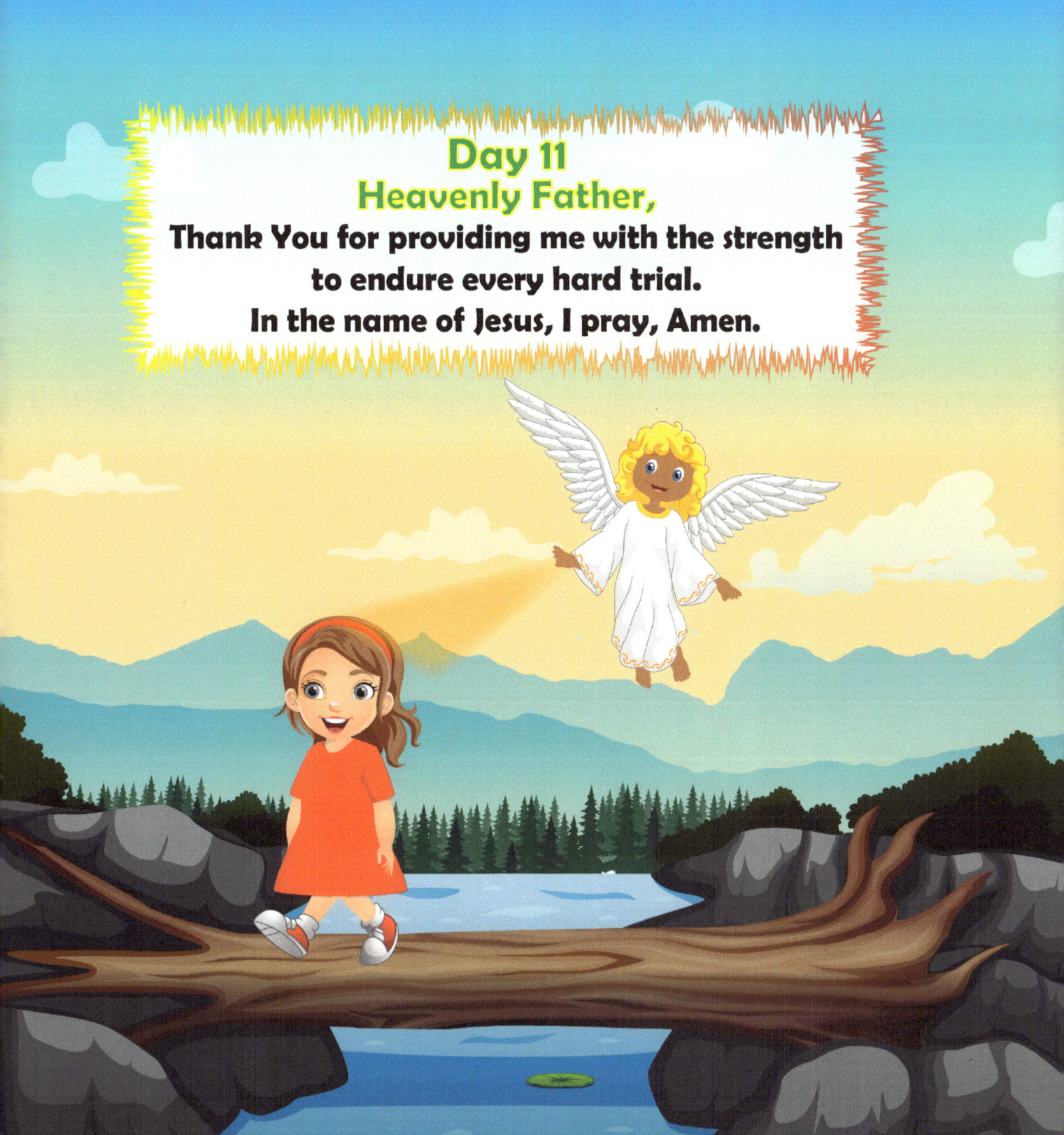

**Day 11**
**Heavenly Father,**
Thank You for providing me with the strength
to endure every hard trial.
In the name of Jesus, I pray, Amen.

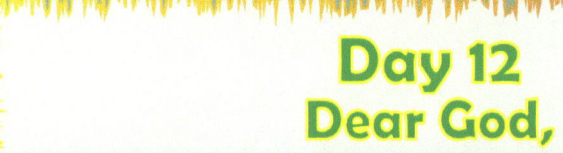

**Day 12**
**Dear God,**
Thank You for blessing me so that I am
a blessing to my family and others.
In the name of Jesus, I pray. Amen.

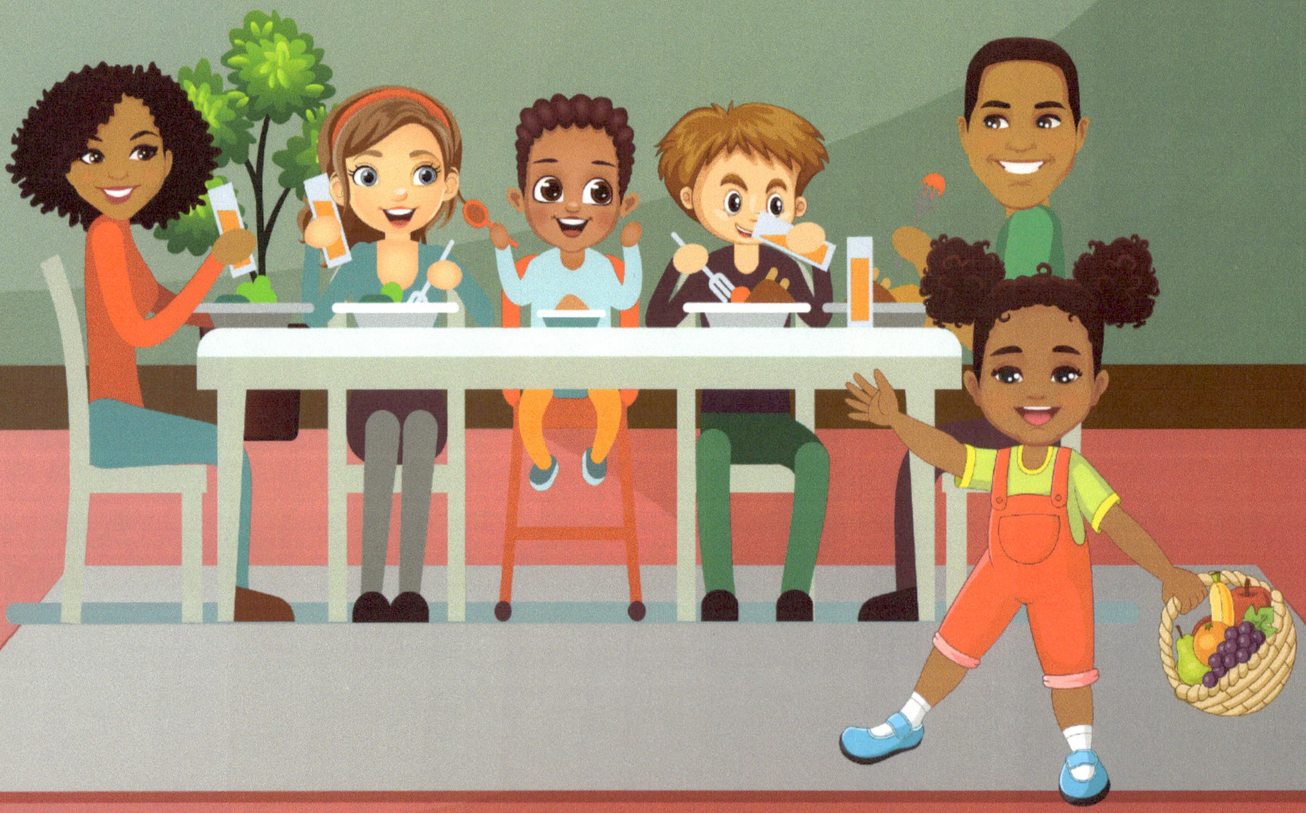

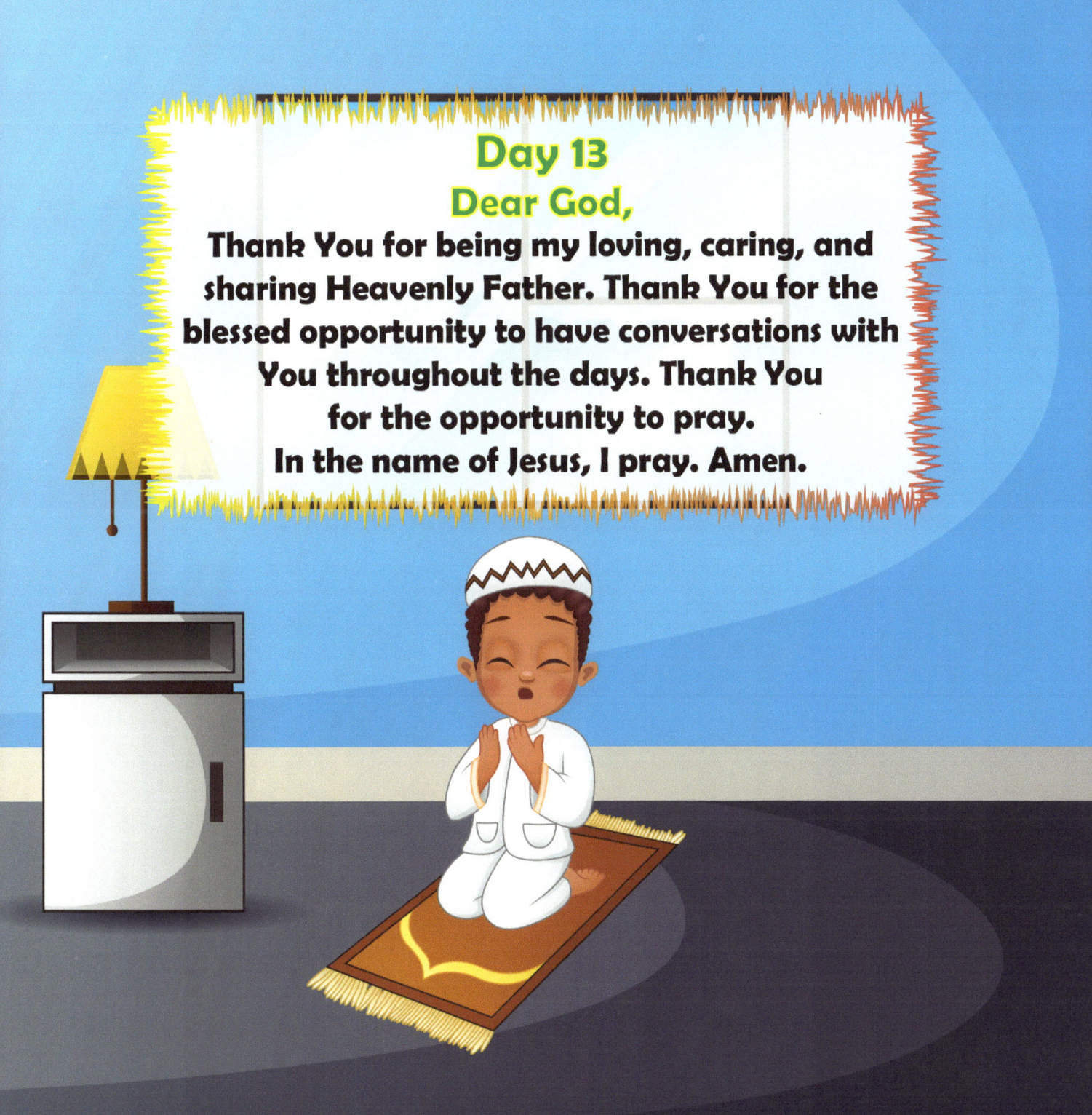

**Day 13**
**Dear God,**
Thank You for being my loving, caring, and sharing Heavenly Father. Thank You for the blessed opportunity to have conversations with You throughout the days. Thank You for the opportunity to pray.
In the name of Jesus, I pray. Amen.

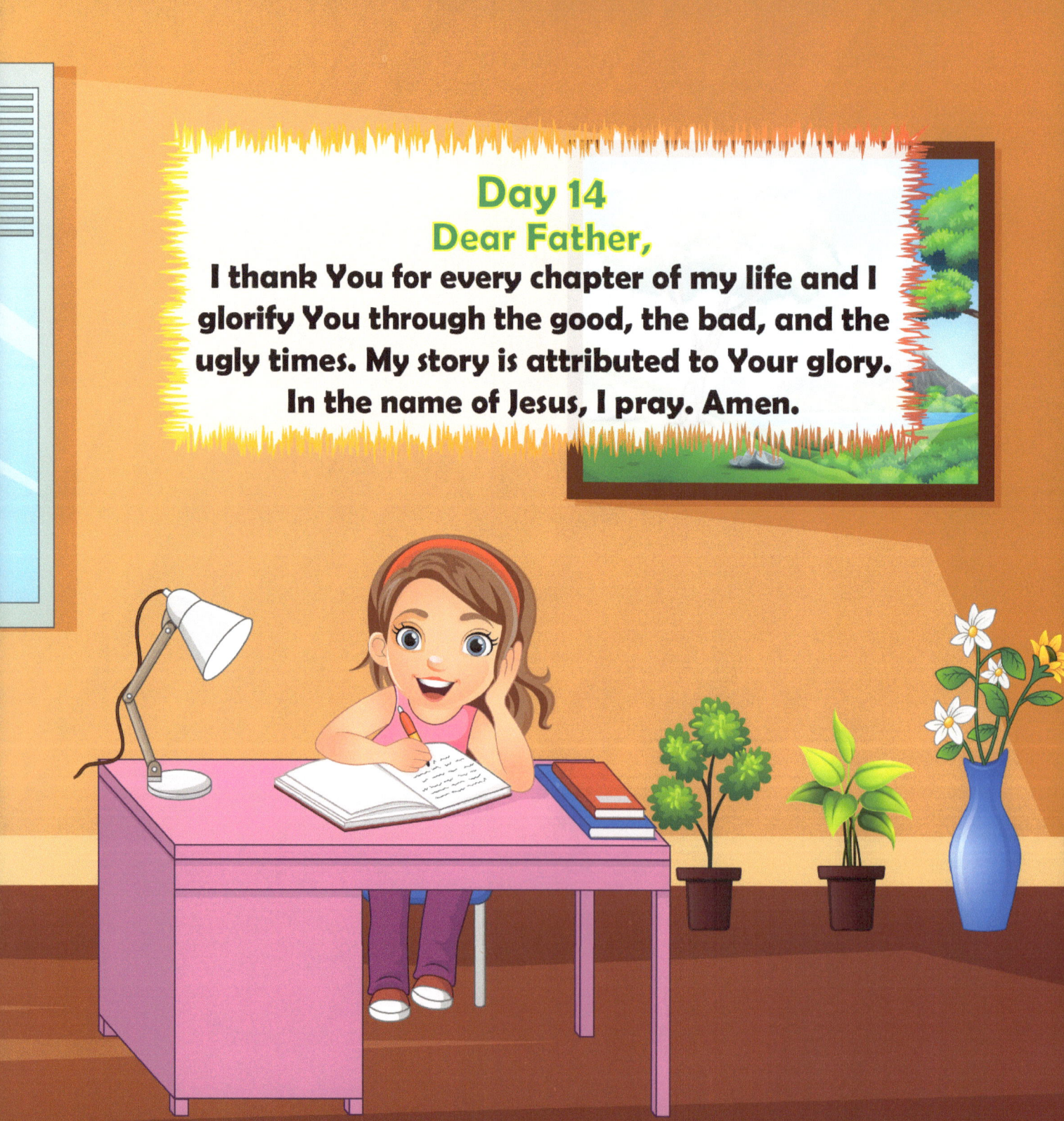

**Day 14**
**Dear Father,**
I thank You for every chapter of my life and I glorify You through the good, the bad, and the ugly times. My story is attributed to Your glory. In the name of Jesus, I pray. Amen.

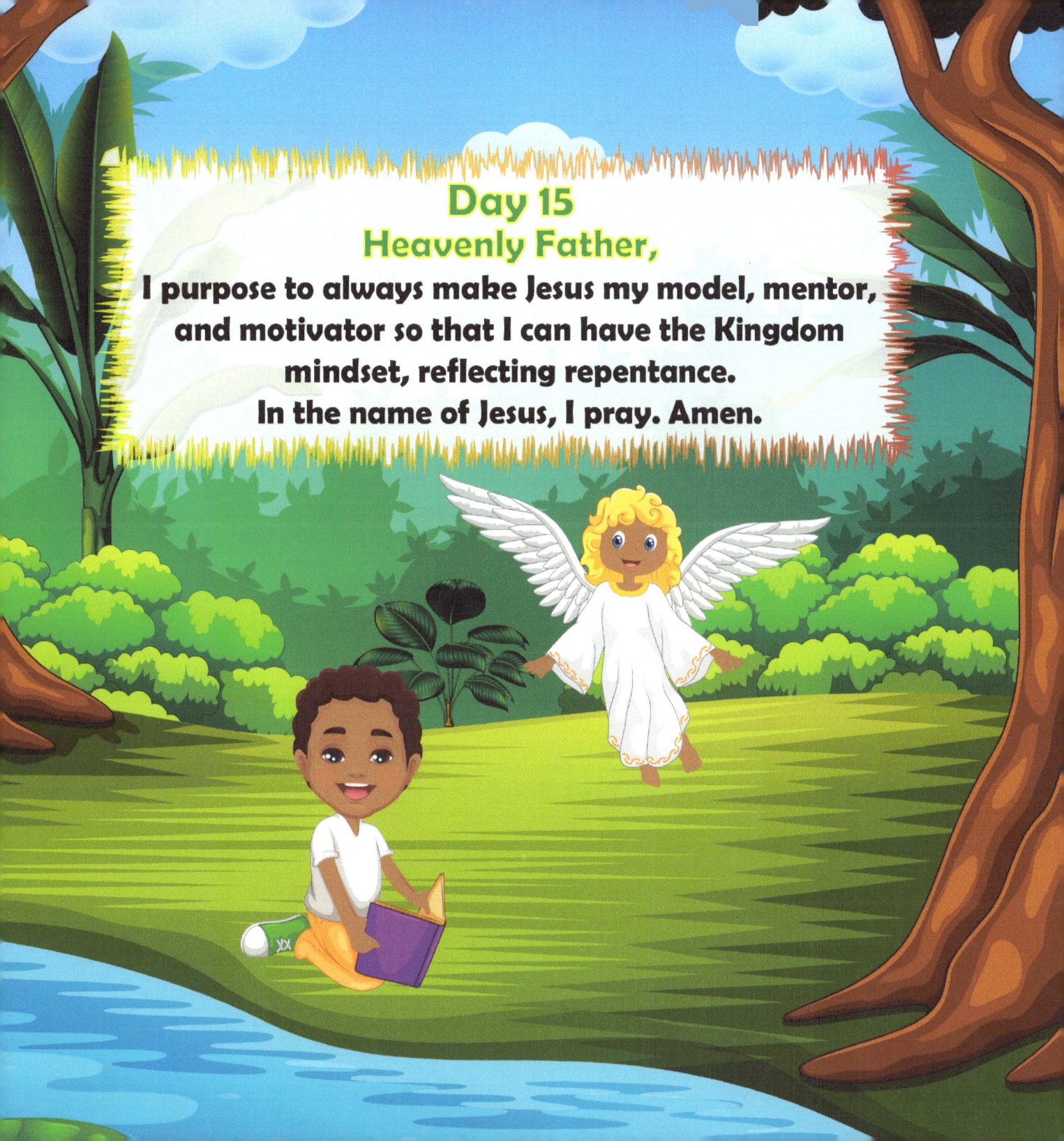

**Day 15**
**Heavenly Father,**
I purpose to always make Jesus my model, mentor, and motivator so that I can have the Kingdom mindset, reflecting repentance.
In the name of Jesus, I pray. Amen.

# Day 16
## Dear Father God,

I declare to the world that You are glorious, and You are worthy to be praised! Thank You for being my loving, caring, and sharing Heavenly Father. In the name of Jesus, I pray. Amen.

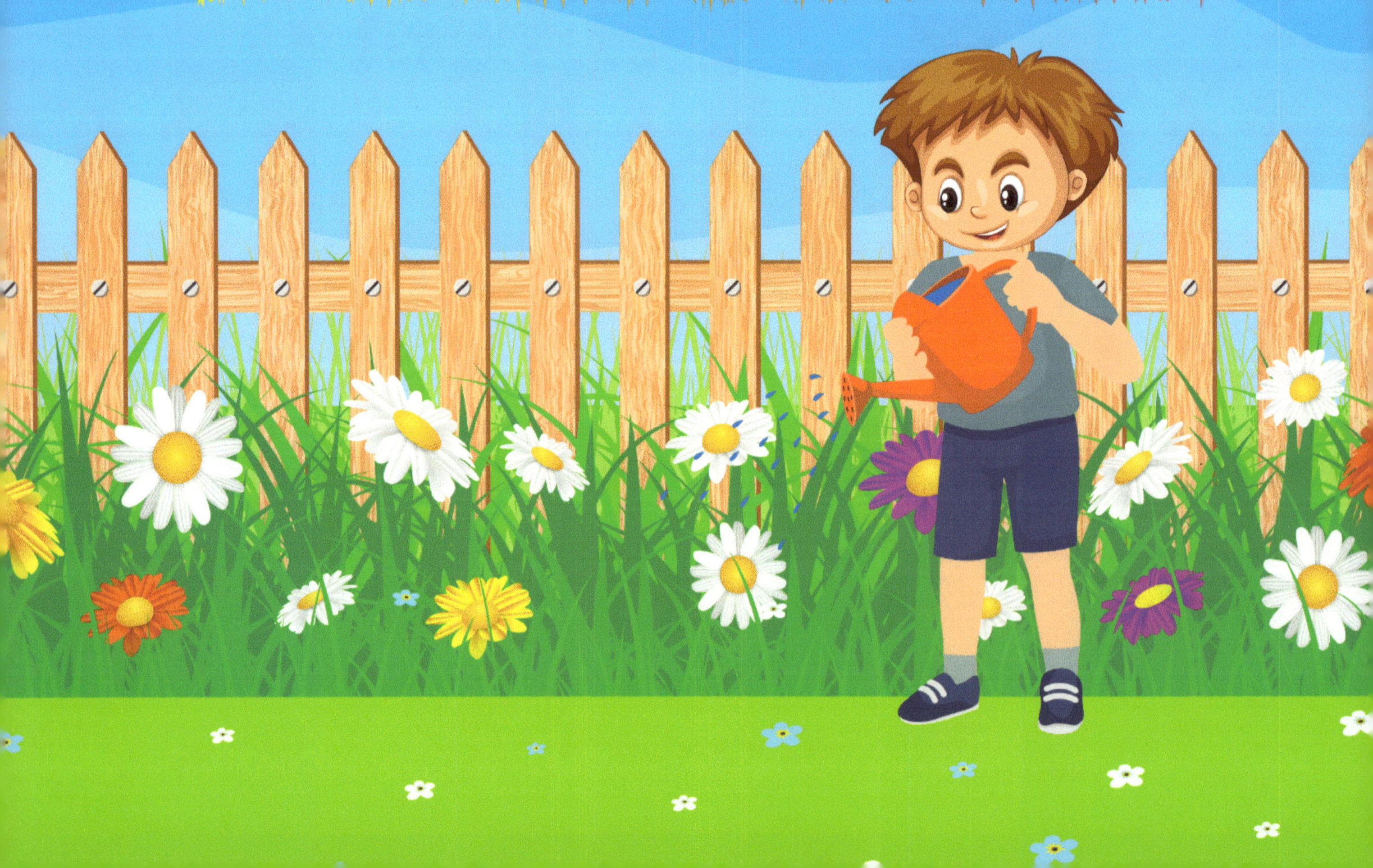

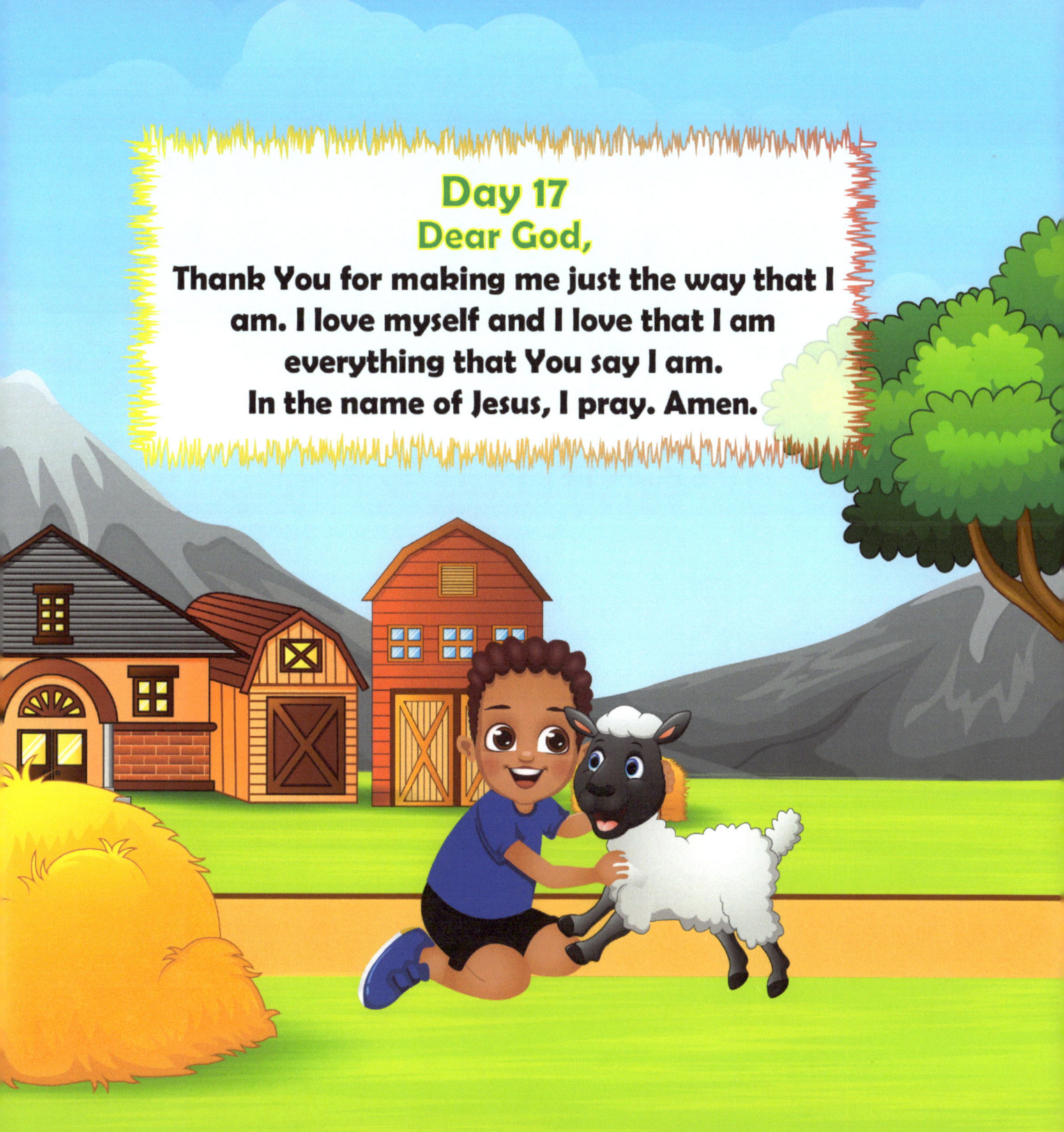

**Day 17**
**Dear God,**
Thank You for making me just the way that I am. I love myself and I love that I am everything that You say I am.
In the name of Jesus, I pray. Amen.

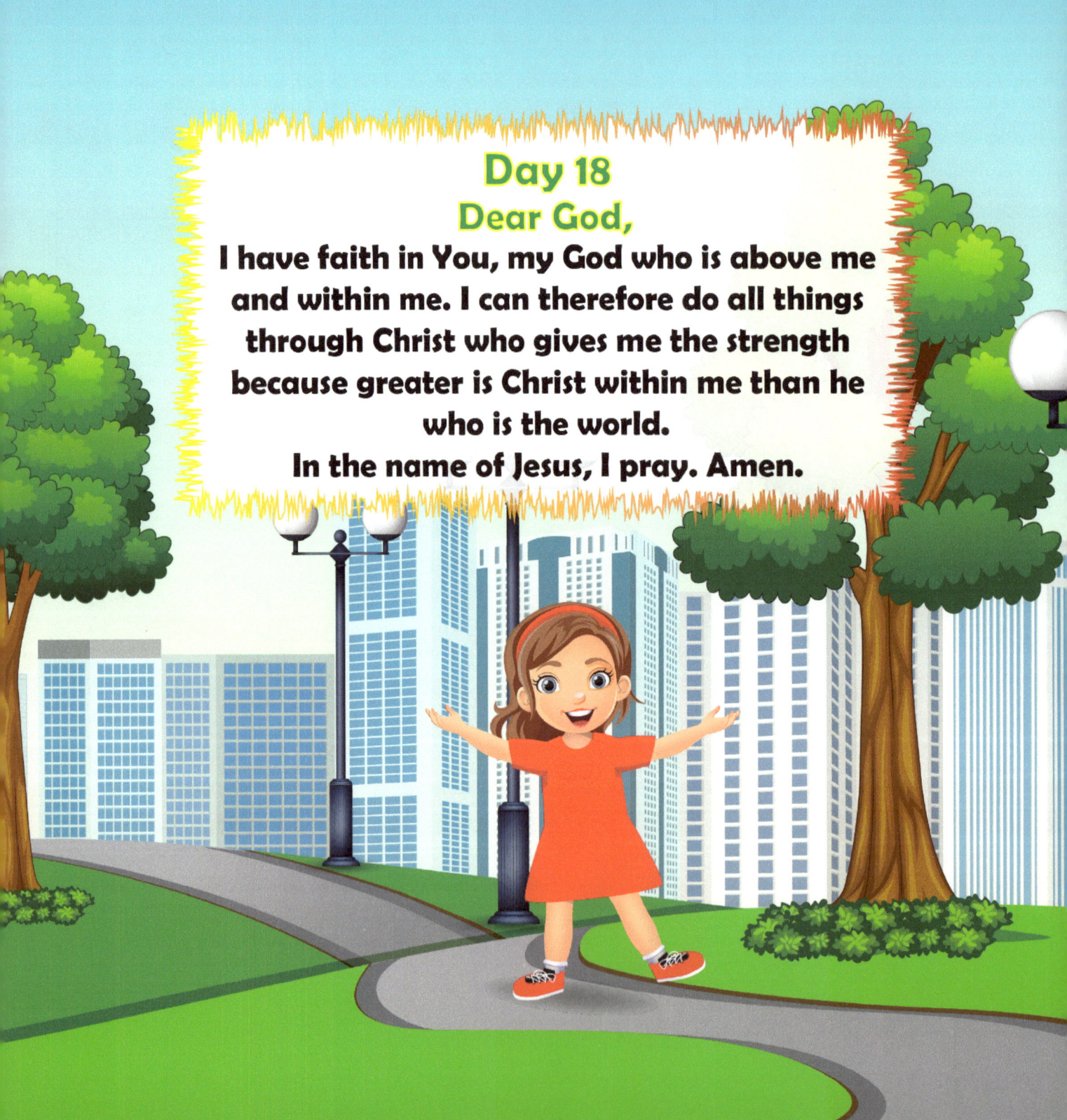

**Day 18**
**Dear God,**
I have faith in You, my God who is above me and within me. I can therefore do all things through Christ who gives me the strength because greater is Christ within me than he who is the world.
In the name of Jesus, I pray. Amen.

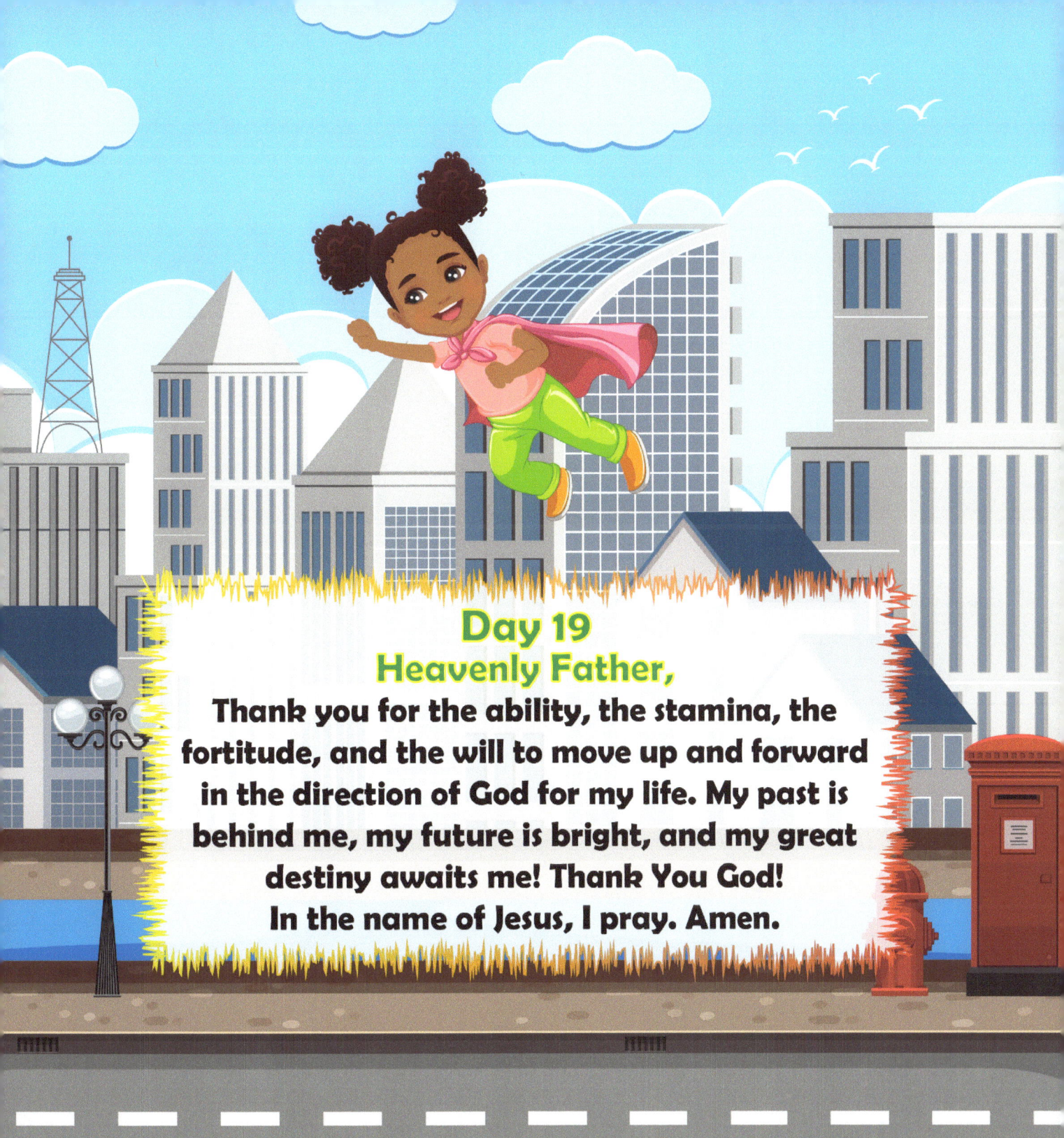

## Day 19
### Heavenly Father,

Thank you for the ability, the stamina, the fortitude, and the will to move up and forward in the direction of God for my life. My past is behind me, my future is bright, and my great destiny awaits me! Thank You God!
In the name of Jesus, I pray. Amen.

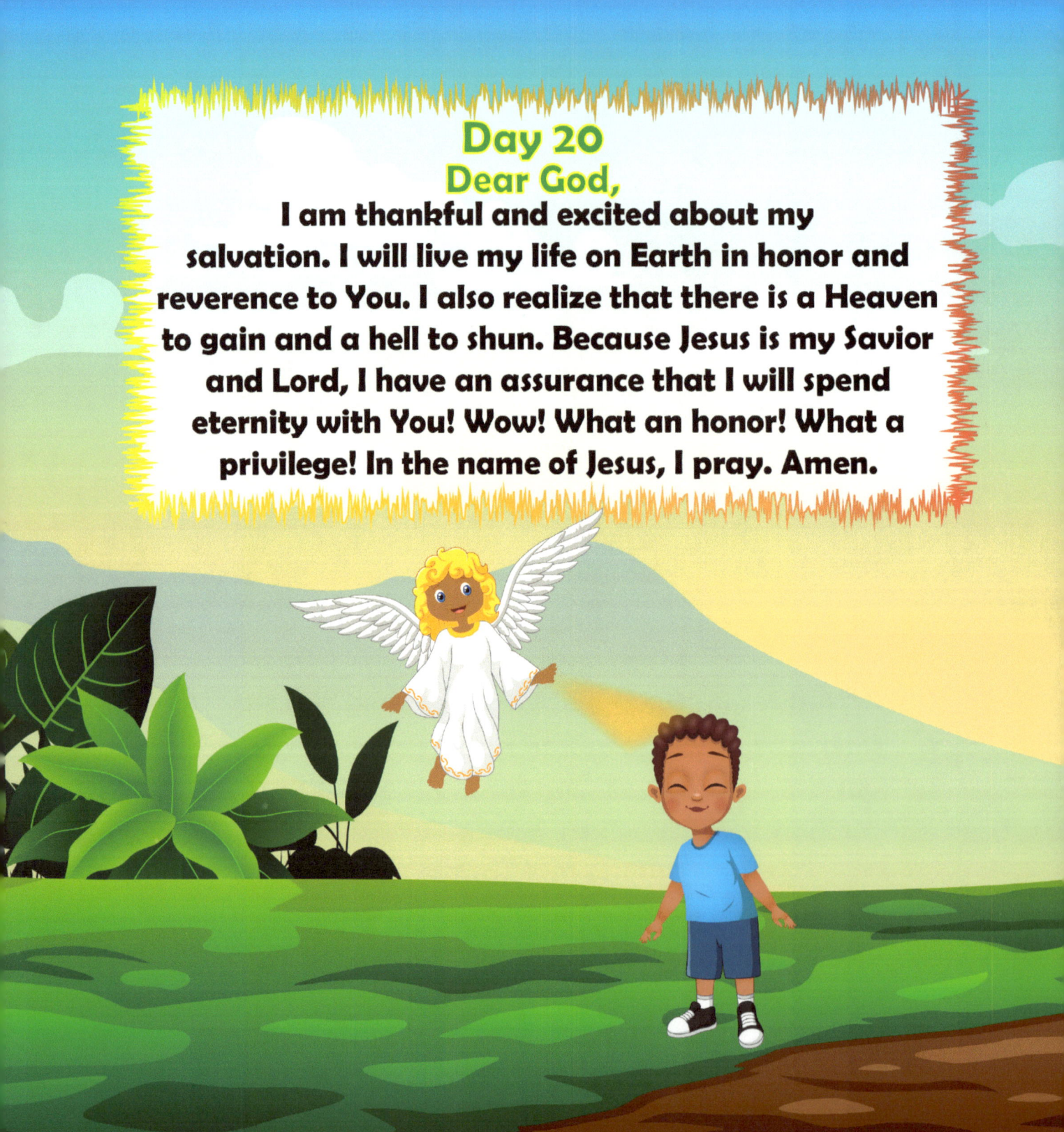

# Day 20
## Dear God,

I am thankful and excited about my salvation. I will live my life on Earth in honor and reverence to You. I also realize that there is a Heaven to gain and a hell to shun. Because Jesus is my Savior and Lord, I have an assurance that I will spend eternity with You! Wow! What an honor! What a privilege! In the name of Jesus, I pray. Amen.

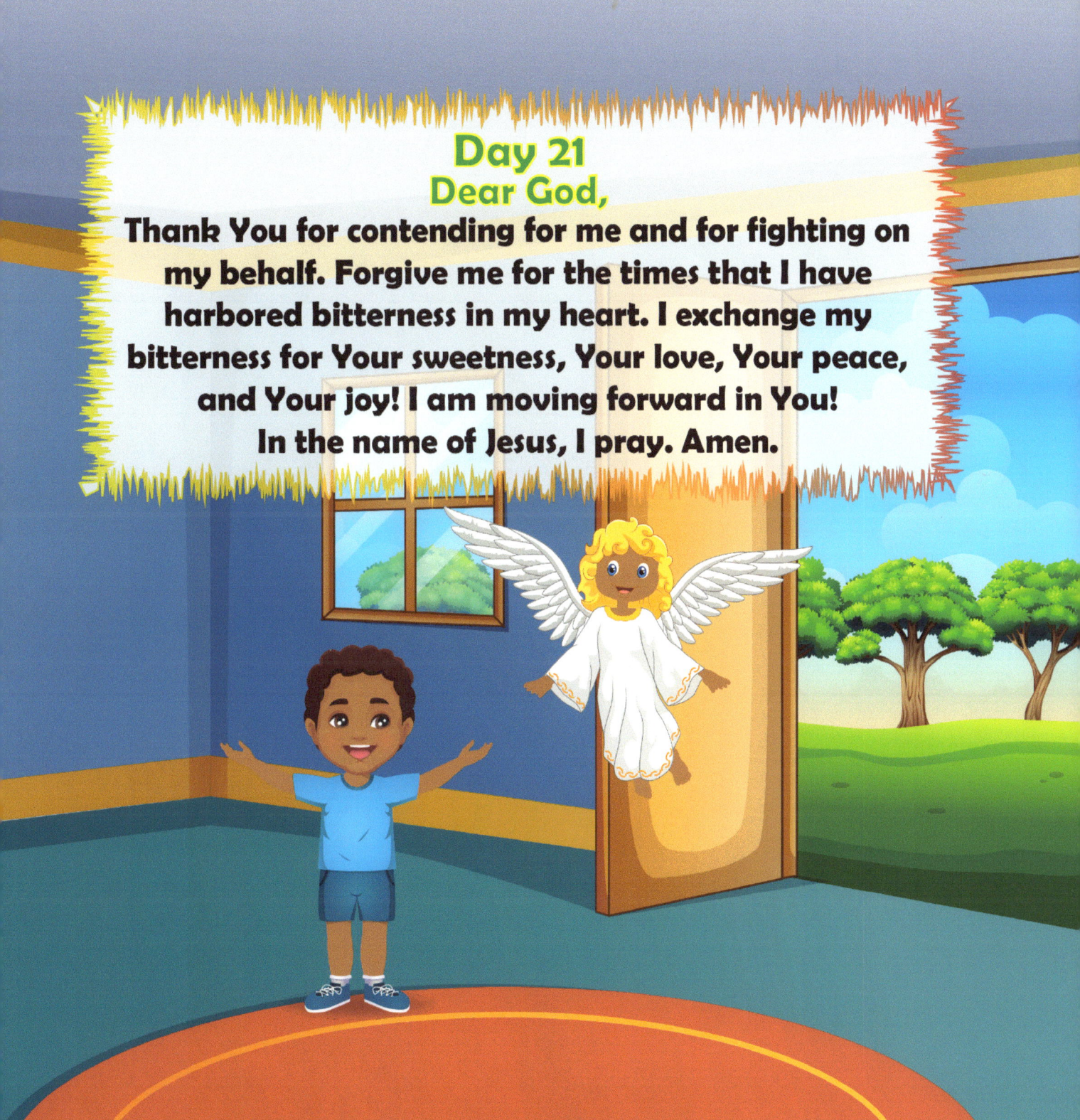

# Day 21
## Dear God,

Thank You for contending for me and for fighting on my behalf. Forgive me for the times that I have harbored bitterness in my heart. I exchange my bitterness for Your sweetness, Your love, Your peace, and Your joy! I am moving forward in You!
In the name of Jesus, I pray. Amen.